My Abundant Universe

prosperity and the path of least resistance

by Arna Baartz

a girl god workbook

ISBN: 978-82-93725-33-6
Copyright 2017 Arna Baartz

arnabaartz.com.au

Praise for New Love

"The title of this powerful book says it all. It truly is a TOOLBOX for undoing all the knots living inside us from this long era of patriarchy. *New Love* could easily be adapted to last more than 30 days, as each day offers so much richness to contemplate and incorporate. Grateful for this divine collaboration between these two powerhouse women! *New Love* will indeed awaken a new love in women the world over."–Melia Keeton-Digby, author of *The Heroines Club*

"If you have an intention to embrace abundance and release yourself from self-limiting narratives, *New Love* is the perfect guide. Here's to a new love that will transform not just women, but the very ground on which we walk."
–Elizabeth Hall Magill, author of *Defining Sexism in the U.S.*

"*New Love* is beautifully written and illustrated with artwork that blends in so nicely with the words. The quotes are reminders of our strengths, growth and wisdom, something we often forget as life and society challenges us. *New Love* allows the platform to free our minds and tune into ourselves."–Alyscia Cunningham, author of *Feminine Transitions*

Praise for The Creative Warrior

"I need no excuse to reach for the felt tip pens and now I get to colour in the work of one of my favourite artists while exploring + healing myself, my creativity + my inner child in this book, *The Creative Warrior.* What Arna offers in these pages are a permission slip to play, to make mistakes and to celebrate your right to make a mark. Warning: once you let Arna and this book awaken your creative child, if you're anything like me, you'll find you will want to colour outside the lines on the page + in life too!" –Lisa Lister, author of *Code Red*

"What lovely invitations Arna's words and drawings are—beckoning us to shimmy out of our adult shells and dance freely with memory, colour, dreams and desires. This is a beautiful book from an inspiring woman who keeps faith with the magic of our creative purpose and understands its gift for keeping us passionately engaged and alive!"
–Melaina Faranda, author of *The Circle* Series

"Hand in hand with your inner child, *The Creative Warrior* invites you into the transformative world of play, joy and whimsy. Be ready to be delighted and empowered as you add color and embellishments to Arna Baartz's stunning, evocative images—and gently guided in your artistic self-discovery through inspirational quotes, creative inquiries and suggested activities. A magical adventure of reclaiming your own creative warrior awaits you!"
–Karen Clark, author of *Tale of the Lost Daughter*

Girl God Books

Re-Membering with Goddess: Healing the Patriarchal Perpetuation of Trauma

An anthology of women's experiences of trauma—trauma as a result of patriarchy; trauma perpetuated by patriarchy; and how through personal healing of trauma the Goddess is re-membered, re-embodied and resurrected.

In Defiance of Oppression - The Legacy of Boudicca

An anthology that encapsulates the Spirit of the defiant warrior in a modern apathetic age. No longer will the voices of our sisters go unheard, as the ancient Goddesses return to the battlements, calling to ignite the spark within each and every one of us—to defy oppression wherever we find it, and stand together in solidarity.

Warrior Queen: Answering the Call of The Morrigan

A powerful anthology about the Irish Celtic Goddess. Each contributor brings The Morrigan to life with unique stories that invite readers to partake and inspire them to pen their own. Included are essays, poems, stories, chants, rituals, and art from dozens of story-tellers and artists from around the world, illustrating and recounting the many ways this powerful Goddess of war, death, and prophecy has changed their lives.

Willendorf's Legacy: The Sacred Body

Travel through time and discover a world where the fullness of women was both admired and deified. Reclaim your beautiful Goddess body through the rich pages of this powerful collection of art, poetry and essays celebrating our divine inheritance as daughters of Willendorf.

Inanna's Ascent: Reclaiming Female Power

Inanna's Ascent examines how females can rise from the underworld and reclaim their power, sovereignly expressed through poetry, prose and visual art. All contributors are extraordinary women in their own right, who have been through some difficult life lessons—and are brave enough to share their stories.

Re-visioning Medusa: from Monster to Divine Wisdom

A remarkable collection of essays, poems, and art by scholars who have researched Her, artists who have envisioned Her, and women who have known Her in their personal story. All have spoken with Her and share something of their communion in this anthology.

On the Wings of Isis: Reclaiming the Sovereignty of Auset

For centuries, women have lived, fought and died for their equality, independence and sovereignty. Originally known as Auset, the Egyptian Goddess Isis reveals such a path. Unfurl your wings and join an array of strong women who have embodied the Goddess of Ten Thousand Names to celebrate their authentic selves.

Mentorship with Goddess: Growing Sacred Womanhood
Mentorship with Goddess is a workbook – a year-long programme – a rite of passage –
especially useful for the transition into autonomous adulthood – and also for the
menopause journey. The programme can be undertaken solo or as a group. The specific aim
is *growing* Sacred Womanhood.

How to Live Well Despite Capitalist Patriarchy
A book challenging societal assumptions to help women become stronger and break free of
their chains.

The Girl God
A book for children young and old, celebrating the Divine Female by Trista Hendren.
Magically illustrated by Elisabeth Slettnes with quotes from various faith traditions and
feminist thinkers.

My Name is Medusa
The story of the greatly misunderstood Medusa, including why she likes snakes. *My Name is
Medusa* explores the "scary" dark side, the potency of nature and the importance of
dreams. Arna Baartz gorgeously illustrates this tale by Glenys Livingstone, teaching children
(big and small) that our power often lies in what we have been taught to fear and revile.

My Name is Inanna
Tamara Albanna weaves the tale of Inanna's despair, strength and triumph—giving children
of all ages hope that the dark times in life will pass. Arna Baartz illustrates this journey with
gorgeous paintings of the owls, lions, stars, sun and moon that direct Her. *My Name is
Inanna* is dedicated to Tamara's beloved homeland, Iraq—The Cradle of Civilization; the
Land of the Goddess.

My Name is Lilith
Whether you are familiar with the legend of Lilith or hearing it for the first time, you will be
carried away by this lavishly illustrated tale of the world's first woman. This creative retelling
of Lilith's role in humanity's origins will empower girls and boys to seek relationships based
on equality rather than hierarchy.

My Name is Isis
A fresh look at the ancient Egyptian Goddess, Susan Morgaine reclaims Isis as The Great
Mother Goddess and The Giver of Life, from whom all things come. Arna Baartz mystically
illustrates Her as healer and protectress. *My Name is Isis* is a treasure box for children of all
ages who want to draw close to this wise and nurturing Mother Goddess.

Additional Offerings by Arna Baartz

New Love: a reprogramming toolbox for undoing the knots

A powerful combination of emotional/spiritual techniques, art and inspiring words for women who wish to move away from patriarchal thought. This reprogramming toolbox combines the wisdom of intentional visual art and inspiring words. *New Love* includes a mixture of compelling thoughts and suggestions for each day, along with a "toolbox" to help you change the parts of your life you want to heal.

THE CREATIVE WARRIOR: A Colouring Journal for Adults to Awaken the Creative Child

So much more than an ordinary colouring in book, *The Creative Warrior* is a journey of personal empowerment. This book has been designed to awaken your inner creative being and gently connect you with your most satisfying and creative self. *The Creative Warrior* blossoms with encouraging quotes, numerous colouring sheets of unique images, suggestions, activities and insightful thoughts. Written and illustrated by Arna Baartz.

I Am Change

Using loving words and creative activities, *I Am Change* provides the tools you need to gently yet powerfully guide you into a new understanding of your world. With strategies to release addiction, dissolve drama and shift perspectives, you will learn to forge a personal path of well-being and prosperity. Coming soon!

The Animals Know It

The Animals Know It is a book designed to remind children of their empowered state of being. Complete with wisdom from the animals—and bright, colourful images and colouring sheets to trigger the imagination—this book will entertain and delight.

The Sun is in my Mouth

A collection of words by Arna Baartz.

arnabaartz.com.au

Dedicated to My Spiritual Partner in Grand Financial Success

Monica Batiste.

Introduction

The change from lack to prosperity thinking can seem impossible, out of reach, or just an irrationally scary concept for many of us—but it can still be what we deeply desire and know we need. We just must find a way to turn the switch from fear of the unknown to expecting something different. We only need to relax enough to allow the abundant universe to turn our fear into an exciting prospect, full of potential and reward.

It has been scientifically shown that we, the thinker/feeler, direct our neural growth. This growth response to emotional and linguistic programming takes as little as 28 days of consistent, conscious effort and can (and does) have dramatic and noticeable effects on our external experience.

This 30-day prosperity program is for the one who wants to take life by the horns and get spirit into action.

For a 30-day intention to work in any obvious way, your commitment is the most important component. For many of my programs, I will suggest you go at your own pace—but for this particular science/magic I say brave it, take the abundant bull by the horns!

The discomfort may be strong but the desire to breathe through and become what you know you can be / must be stronger.

Whatever your desired outcome for this 30-day process you need to have faith that everything you are doing is exactly right—and that you are being guided, loved, and supported at all times. If you become distracted, that's OK, just get right back on your horse as soon as you realise. Once you have started there really is no going back—every little action/relaxation counts!

Make deep connections between your thoughts and your external world wherever you can, and notice synchronicity at every turn. Do not be afraid of taking full responsibility on a spiritual level for what occurs in your experience. This is the way of the soul warrior; to realign the self with your power as a deliberate and joyful creator.

Approaching an intention like this with the specific desire to change needs to be done with clarity of purpose and with awareness and flexibility. We must consider that any habit or concept we wish to change has become a distinct part of our being and we are now used to living with it. This means that as we move into a new state of being we will feel certain emotions and resistances arise.

To affect change in a 30-day period you must be aware of the resistance as it arises and have the courage to feel the feelings it brings with it, then turn again and again to your set of tools to keep you focused on your new desire.

Also be aware that after you have made an intention—such as, 'I choose to see my life as abundant'—your powerful mind will lead you down the path of least resistance. That could result in finding yourself in seemingly undesirable situations. For example, your purse may be temporarily empty, and you will be forced to relax anyway and look around for unusual alternatives.

When this happens for me, I remind myself—this must be the most efficient path to awareness. If I take the time for personal inquiry, I will no doubt find a connection between the situation and my desire to live differently.

If you are asking for more time, more money, or more love—you must be willing to notice all the tiny steps that occur in your external world. If you really want to change, you don't get to dismiss these moments as random or coincidental anymore. The more you acknowledge the tiny miracles, the more they will grow. If you have asked for more money, pick up that 5-cent piece you see and thank your mind for its powerful focusing ability—and your new money- attracting vibration. By the same token, if you should suddenly get a great big, unexpected bill—notice it and say, 'I did this! This is an opportunity for me to take a calm and focused look at the way I view/spend/attract money.'

Be willing to adjust your intention—from 'I want to have more money' to 'I am willing to understand my relationship to money today.' Sometimes it will be necessary to ask an extra question or become curious about the way your belief system has been carrying and directing you so far.

I always like to make my intention—say it is 'I wish to make more money'—and then add at the end something like, 'In the easiest, safest, and most joyful way possible.' This is just in case I have a belief system that says change is scary or dangerous—so I don't activate my fear and get in my own way.

At the end of the process, if you follow these instructions, you will notice change. You will find yourself—at the very least—in the beginning stages of a true and powerful awakening.

As the new burst of energy comes into your body, it will be your job to become sensitive to it—to encourage it, to breathe through it—and to surrender if it is stronger than you may have thought you were ready for. Nothing comes to you without your approval and your readiness. But you must remember that you are the commander, and you can take control of your process whenever necessary through simple words and relaxation.

Enjoy this journey and stay focused on emotional awareness, self-love, and oneness as your ultimate, expanding goal.

Remember this is a life journey—it doesn't end after thirty days. You will continue to grow and evolve and expand upon your intentions—and even though sometimes you may feel at a standstill, this won't be the case—it will just be a short breather as your old fluff drops off and a new perspective forms.

If you choose to stop your personal development after thirty days, you will still have moved and changed your mind deliberately. And that, in and of itself, is awesome!

I Move with the Flow of this Abundant Universe

MONEY

Affluence
Currency
Flow
Movement
Energy
Life

I AM a constant vibrating connected cell of this flushed and abundant universe.

Arna Baartz

How to Use this Book

My Abundant Universe is an immediate experience, created to help you gain a deep understanding of what it takes to make conscious positive change as quickly as possible for you.

In this book, we are leaping at the opportunity to explore our relationship with money. We are taking an unabashed look at the values we hold that either attract or repel prosperity.

One of the key components to adjusting your receptivity to prosperity is to enhance ease and grace wherever and whenever possible in your daily experience. In this book, you will find quotes from wise people who have understood that relaxation is the quickest way to success— and you will experience written flows of abundance designed to spark a sense of joy, enthusiasm, and hope. These expressive paragraphs use a diversity of subject matter to flick on your abundance switch. There are colourful images to spark the visual receptors in your magnificent brain and inspire your own creativity, opening you to more in that department. You are given important journaling space to contemplate questions specifically related to your prosperity belief systems, explore your resistance, release your fear and graphically visualise your desire.

Call it what you will—financial abundance, material success, prosperity, wealth, riches—we can release our investment, put rest to our shame, and embrace our truth. With intention and diligent awareness we will—once again—see our natural right of way, gaining conscious access to the abundant universe.

I hope to set the waves of potential in motion—and help the intellectual and visual among us to have those light bulb moments necessary for the brain to latch on and evolve an idea.

So read the words and quotes from people who have made their own magnificent discoveries— feel the feelings and journal your thoughts.

You might choose to sketch and draw, collage or simply write down what comes to mind.

Make sure you question everything—especially if you feel you don't agree with what you are reading. Write it down and explore the debate; these are powerful steps in the direction of change. If you don't feel good reading something in this book you can always make the powerful choice to skip it and find something to read or do that makes your heart radiate with happiness.

Feel free to write all over the book. This is your diary—use it as a friend make your intentions clear and celebrate your potential!

This workbook can also be utilized in women's circles—or in a private online community with Girl God Books. It often helps to have an accountability partner or group! Contact support@girlgod.org for discounts on bulk orders or information about current online offerings. Consider these words by Sedonia Cahill:

"My women's lodge has been meeting for over fifteen years and we've talked about many topics, including aging and death. We spent several meetings telling our sexual history from beginning to end. With that topic we were all able to laugh and cry together as we discovered that the telling of these stories wasn't hard to do. Then we decided to talk about money. In the first evening it was amazing to find that this group of very competent women had so much shame and embarrassment talking about it. We had no difficulty in our meetings about sex, or death. But money was hard to talk about.

There were tears as we told stories revealing how mystifying money was to each of us. Somehow, we hadn't been raised to understand it. We had mismanaged our own money, lost money, and almost never asked for the amount of money we deserved for our work. There was guilt about having money, guilt about not having money. For middle-class women of our generation, talking about money had been a family taboo. We stayed with this subject for several meetings because it was so potent, and each time I dreaded going to the circle, thinking, "I really don't want to face this." After that, each woman in the group took various steps to get a handle on the issue. I know I did. **Those circles changed our lives**."

Every Day Remembering

I need to list a few key points here, things to remember each day. One of the reasons you are wanting or doing anything in life—including this prosperity course—is so that you can feel better than you already do.

Feel better—it is all about feelings!

We are on this earth as sensitive, sensual beings. We want to feel good, we want to eat, sleep, be with each other in great feeling ways. The issue is this: although this is who we really are, life has become confusing and falsely stimulating so we have lost connection with our own emotional body.

Remember each day to come back into your body, to feel the sensations of the present moment and know that above all else, your main intention is to feel good.

PRESENCE: What can I do to become more present and relaxed?

TRUST: What can I do to enhance the trust and faith in my universe to provide?

LOVE: How do I broaden my perspective on LOVE as the energy that brings life to all things?

DEVOTION: Can I devote my day to seeing abundance everywhere I look?

CONNECTION: Where can I relax, centre myself and connect sincerely throughout my day today?

ENERGY: How can I bring energy to my cells today? Breath, nourishment, movement…?

Money is like love—and our relationship to the 'Godhead' has a lot to do with how much we are letting into our lives. From the get-go, we tend to personify 'GOD' and in doing so we replace an all loving, vibrant universal, and genderless mind, with what we know of 'the father' archetype.

The way I see it is that all life trauma works to cloud our perspective, fogs up our 'windows', and impedes our sense of connection with a genuine and limitless supply of energy.

Our work becomes about learning to feel again and to see with clarity, giving in to trust as we test the water with our big toe.

Little by little, we relax enough to feel our emotion while consciously present—letting our cells soften and our system release the tight hold on judgement and expectation.

We are like a hurt and frightened child, unwilling to look a friend in the eye even though they offer only love and good intentions. Moment by moment if the friend persists in a loving, non-judgemental state, regardless of the child's fear and connection to memory and pain, the child will trust again.

So we move into a state of grace turning our face toward the universe and—whoosh!—the abundance of love, energy, money comes flowing toward us.

In a timely, quantum move, we re-establish the flow of universal energy with our simple attention to it.

It is crucial to remember that although we have intentions to change our mindset and allow our perspective to shift, we are still here and now, experiencing the reality we have expected thus far. To change we must accept our pivotal point, and that is this moment NOW.

This is IT. THIS is it. This IS it.

Understanding and accepting this moment means forgiving the past, diverting our attention from it whenever we can, and feeling the feelings when they come up.

It means taking responsibility for all our choices so far.

You don't have to do anything except get it, sit with it and say, *I did this, here I am, this is it and I am OK.*

Day One

Although this book is written with an abundance focus, you are welcome to use it to unlock your grip on a different sector of your life.

The whole concept behind opening the flow of abundance incorporates all aspects of the system.

We can focus our thoughts on money and activate a tight feeling of resistance in any number of areas. The trick to gaining positive momentum in prosperity consciousness is to become aware of resistance as it comes up, no matter what the subject.

Turn it into a game—spend a moment with each of the thoughts below and journal what comes up for you immediately—is it a resistant reaction, tightness in your body, negative thought or a feeling of ease, motivation, or excitement?

Example List

Money

Time

Health

Happiness

Love

Past

Taking an inventory of your immediate reaction to these few simple words will give you an indication of what is going on in your mind.

You can see clearly whether you are in the habit of resistance and negativity or if you are hopeful and positive in your general thoughts.

Choosing the subjects you feel less resistant to as your *go-to* subjects when training the brain to become easier about life will help you journey into an abundant flow.

When you feel a resistant thought come into your mind—breathe deeply, relax your body, feel the feeling, and intend to release it.

Then find a thought that ignites a more positive neural response; your puppy, the sky, a colour, someone you like—or focus on an activity that makes you feel better: walk, dance, cook or read. This isn't distraction. This is feeling your feelings and changing the path your current neurons are developing in your brain.

This is self-responsibility and empowerment. If you want to be abundant, first you must regain your sense of power and self-worth—and you must find a way to feel abundant despite the reality you may be living.

Now state your intention out loud, clearly, and with feeling.

Examples

I would like more money, in the easiest, safest, and most joyful way for me.

I am willing to allow myself to attract money, safely and joyfully.

I wish to see continuing evidence of this happening in the next thirty days.

I would like to see, understand and change my values around money.

Feel the words until you come up with something just right.

Repeat your intention every day, feeling into the words and adjusting the intention accordingly. Keep the focus on curiosity and positive expectation.

Each day I will give you a simple task and a new concept to play with and if you stay on the path your intention will begin manifesting immediately. Remember that manifestation starts as an emotional template and builds into form from there, becoming more solid and true as you gain positive momentum in your mind!

An Abundance of Sensational Sky

I feel sky, I see sky, there is an absolute abundance of sky.

I always have enough sky!

Beautiful shades of delicious sky, delightful blue, stormy purple and grey,
lolly-pop pink, red and orange.

Sky inspires me, covers me, protects me, speaks to me.

Every day I wake up to the sky, an abundance of sky,
enough wonderful nurturing sky for us all!

The sky holds magic, it fills me with wonder and delight,
I am in a dome of wealthy sky.

I am prosperous with sky.

I am abundant with what the sky brings to my life.

I feel satisfied with the miraculous nature of sky!

Journal Your Thoughts

Q. What is the first word that comes to mind when you think of money?

"How beautiful it is to do nothing, and then to rest afterward."

Spanish Proverb

Repeat your intention out loud, write your intention in your journal, watch your words form, and see the magic today.

Think about what your intention means to you.

Feel into it, how does it feel to you now?

Feel the feelings that repeating the intention bring up for you.

This is a choice you are making. You are a powerful creator in command of your emotional world and your deliberately chosen path forward.

Do you feel positive about your intention?

It doesn't matter; just note whatever feelings are there and decide to do this anyway.

Breathe in deeply and exhale. Make the choice again and again today, 'Yes, this is what I want, I choose this!'

State your intention as often as you remember today. Write it on your hand if you need to. Keep a smile on your face and warmth in your heart. Always exhale any difficult thoughts and feelings and return to the warm 'now' as soon as you can.

Feel The Flow

The flow is like light. It starts with a tingling in my toes
and as I breathe deeply, I feel it spread in silver waves,
cascading stars over my body.

Energy is brushing my skin—
I feel the breath of the universe.

'Abundance' she whispers.

I am cloaked in riches.
Every cell divides in little bursts of joy.
Mirth dances from my eyes.

Success streams, pouring like water, bathing my open heart.

I spread my arms and love twinkles like fireflies from my palms, spreading like
honey
gold
money
throughout my life,
filling every corner.

I am alive.
I am here.
I am.

Journal Your Thoughts

Q. Do you remember what it felt like to receive money as a child?

"Flowers . . . have a mysterious and subtle influence
upon the feelings, not unlike some strains of music.
They relax the tenseness of the mind, they dissolve its rigour."

Henry Ward Beecher

Day Three

Repeat your intention out loud. Write your intention in your journal, watch your words form, and see the magic here.

Has your intention shifted since you thought of it on day one?

This can happen. Go with the flow and allow it to shift into a place that feels comfortable for you.

Please note: if you feel terrible each time you think about your intention, you are alerting yourself to resistance or old unnecessary belief systems you have running. There are a couple of things you can do.

Go straight to the feeling. Sit and feel; track the feelings as they move through your body, journal your thoughts around the subject as they arise.

When you are satisfied for now, take a few deep breaths; exhale, and state your intention again.

Make sure to find as much calm and soothing around the subject as you can. Try statements like, 'Even though it may seem impossible, this world is a miraculous place—I am open to seeing what my mind, in conjunction with this mysterious universe, is capable of.'

If it is too hard to think about your intention and feel good, make a new intention for now—something along the lines of 'I choose to feel better about my intention and to open to my power.'

The next important piece is to focus on something (anything) that feels great. Stay there as long as possible and create the space for the universe to work its non-resistant magic.

Play with the words of your intention again today and when you feel right, state it with further determination.

Keep in mind that you are sending a powerful vibrational message and even though you may not know for sure this will work, you are leaving a space for allowing the seemingly impossible.

Close your eyes and imagine your brain lit up like a city—and shining above is a neon sign with *'I AM Beautiful, Abundant and Worthy'* written in bright sparkling letters.

Breathe out and relax your body whilst focusing on your sign.

Whenever you remember today, close your eyes and see your neon sign. This gives the reprogramming a bit of boost and helps the new set of neurons begin to fire.

Beautiful Abundance of Skin

There is so much skin on me!

I have skin on my arms and legs—great, supple, protective skin.

I have soft skin on my underbelly,
skin on my face, skin skin.

Everywhere I look I see skin!

I am made of soft yummy skin.

This world is abundant in skin, all different shades of gorgeous skin.

Oh, how prosperous we are in beautiful skin, it keeps us secure and safe, it makes us feel
healthy, and it helps to guide us with its intuitive ability to sense things.

Oh, delicious baby skin so soft!

And the amazing quality of a child's skin, translucent and glowing with health.

There is so much skin!

The children's skin, my partner's warm cloak of skin,
my own wonderful skin.

I will have access to the wonder of my skin for the rest of my life!

Oh, SKIN you flow, and you glow, skin skin.

I am wealthy in skin.

There are 7 billion skins in the world—so much skin and enough to go around!

Extra skin on my neck and knees too!

Journal Your Thoughts

Q. When you say the words, 'Money comes easily to me'—how does it feel in your body?

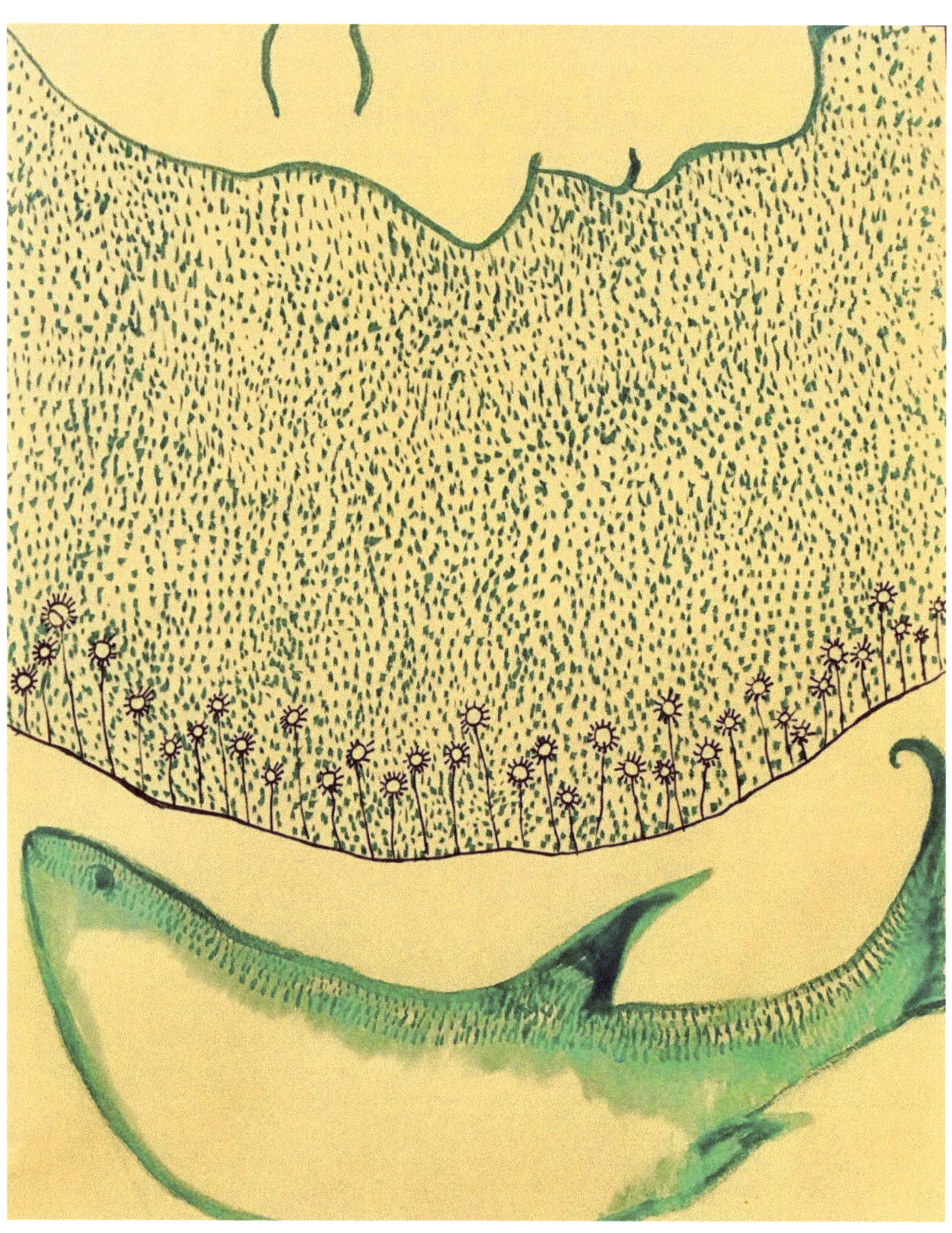

"Envisioning the end is enough to put the means in motion."

Dorothea Brande

Repeat your intention out loud. Write your intention in your journal, watch your words form, and see the magic here.

Can you imagine your life once your intention for prosperity becomes a physical manifestation?

See it in as much detail as you can.

It doesn't matter if you feel you are making it up—that's what powerful creators do.

Write it down as though it has already come into being. Pepper your story with truths from your current reality. The universe doesn't differentiate, it just responds to vibration, and this is one way of adding that smack of truth to something you might think of as a fantasy.

Imagine it and let yourself feel excited about what you see.

Remember, your mind is only capable of imagining a tiny portion of what is possible for you so it is important you leave space for all the other magnificent bits and pieces that will manifest the whole.

Also, know that the universe has only the best in mind for you and is answering your wish as you make it. Your job is to relax and allow it to come into view.

In AM affirmations work best when they are close to what we actually believe and before they present as true in our external lives, they will do their duty to pull up any obstacles in our way.

For example, *I AM A wealthy person* will first highlight why you may believe you are not a wealthy person. This is a GOOD and necessary part of the process to unlock your secret, sabotaging belief systems, welcome this. And even celebrate it allowing curiosity to become part of the game as we open ourselves ready to receive. Be ABUNDANT in curiosity and compassion for yourself as you meet you in a new way.

Sometimes it is great to open the dialogue from a different angle. Take a moment to exclaim 'YOU are beautiful, abundant and worthy! You!' As though you're speaking with love and wonder to yourself, or perhaps your inner child as you make a pact not to abandon or speak negatively to yourself any longer.

Another fabulous technique, which we will be sure to unpack more deeply in our follow up book is to pop a little question into your process. Journaling to yourself like this, with a why. "*WHY* am I so prosperous? How did I become this successfully abundant, home owning queen with a fabulously healthy body and an adoring partner?" Then let your subconscious show you in myriad ways, in your everyday life, with new ideas, via your behaviours, discoveries and encounters. All you have to do is make a personal pact to be observant, kind to yourself and interested in what comes up to be explored.

Prompt for Envisioning

For example:

My home is wonderful!
Describe it in detail here, remember to savor the imagination process and speak in present tense.

My ____ is wonderful!
Describe it in detail here, remember to savor the imagination process and speak in present tense.

My ____ is wonderful!
Describe it in detail here, remember to savor the imagination process and speak in present tense.

My ____ is wonderful!
Describe it in detail here, remember to savor the imagination process and speak in present tense.

My ____ is wonderful!
Describe it in detail here, remember to savor the imagination process and speak in present tense.

My ____ is wonderful!
Describe it in detail here, remember to savor the imagination process and speak in present tense.

My ____ is wonderful!
Describe it in detail here, remember to savor the imagination process and speak in present tense.

Feel The Flow

Feel the warmth trickling through your body.

Experience the tingle of life, the oxygen that slides in between every cell,
punctuating each moment with a climax of YES!

Life is abundant, life is exciting, life is dramatic.

Repeat
I am alive
I am breathing
I am present
I am here
I feel
I see
I taste
I touch

I breathe in the fragrance of jasmine, frangipani, and roses.

I am a wo/man.

This is it.

I am abundant in all things good.

I am excited to be living now with so many opportunities, so many possibilities!
I draw them close into my experience; success is tangible for me—
abundance is imminent.

It is here, it is happening every day.

I am making connections, growing my abundance, practicing my smile.

I am so wealthy with potential—
wealthy in love.

I am flowing with happiness.

Journal Your Thoughts

Q. If I said, 'Here is all the money you can spend but you must only spend it on yourself,' how would that make you feel?

"Tension is who you think you should be. Relaxation is who you are."

Chinese Proverb

Day Five

Repeat your intention out loud. Write your intention in your journal, watch your words form, and see the magic here.

The words "I AM" are the most powerful words we have. In truth, these words have been used throughout history as an incantation of a kind, a way to connect with or name the 'divine.'

In my work I see the words I AM as a powerful reminder of who we are, a piece of the whole, an integral and unwavering spark of All That Is.

I AM is an absolute connection.

I AM is a statement of the highest intention and—when backed up by a sense of knowing and undeterred passion—will produce astounding results.

Bring your intention into the now. Practice wording it *I AM* and see how it feels.

As you practice interchanging your intentions with 'I AM' and 'I WISH,' you will come to feel the powerful difference between a wanting statement and a NOW statement.

The more you say it the more you will sense how real it feels—giving you an opportunity to look into any resistance you feel around the subject.

Practicing feeling the words I AM helps us to find the piece of us that believes in our own creative ability.

An Abundance of Fresh Food

I have an abundance of food—so much we can feed chickens, make compost,
and share with a neighbor.

We are so rich in food and every day, even more food comes into our bags, our home, our
fridge, and cupboards. There is a huge wealth of food in my life.

There is red, yellow, green, and blue food.
There is a rainbow spectrum of food, glorious food, hot sausage, and mustard!

We have food growing in our garden—people bring unexpected food to our door.

Food is tasty and nutritious. It is fuel and I love it.

I love food! I love getting more food! I love sharing food!
I love creating food in a million different ways.
There are so many ways for us to experience food!

We are rich in FOOD. We are prosperous in food and money. We are so wealthy,
we have food driving toward us in trucks right now!

Food is being unloaded as we speak and stocked neatly on the shelves.

We have farmers collecting food for us and offering it to us fresh and beautifully wrapped.

We are the receivers of an abundance of food, love, money, and water!

I expect more food easily every day for fun, for energy—for no reason at all!

Journal Your Thoughts

Q. If Money were a fruit, what colour would it be? What would it taste like?

"I love sloth. I wish sloth would come home and visit me once in a while.
I don't consider laziness a sin at all."

Kajol

Repeat your intention out loud. Write your intention in your journal, watch your words form, and see the magic here.

Use today to introduce a few minutes of quiet time in the morning and the evening. Use this time to notice what you are thinking in relation to your intention.

Breathe deeply and allow yourself to relax into your chair or bed. State your intention and ask yourself, 'what do I really feel about this?'

Then listen, stay focused on your breathing, and allow thoughts to pop up.

You will receive some interesting insight to play with.

You may have to feel some uncomfortable feelings—but then come back to your intention and say, 'Even though I may have resistance, I choose to change, easily and joyfully.'

Notice your breath as you journey through your day. Isn't the exhalation a satisfying experience?

Feel The Flow

The air is alive,
it sparkles with an abundance of intelligent light.

Every breath is satisfying,
wealthy with particles of life.

We share the golden rays of sun,
swimming in delight.

Floating on waves of abundance,
we surrender to universal flow.

Feeling rich with positive expectation and enjoying anticipation,
we receive the bounty!

People are seeking their best selves, looking for answers
and we have them in a multitude of beautiful forms.

We overflow with the love of the universe, the only answer
we could ever need.

We feel wonderful!

Expansion is inevitable.

Journal Your Thoughts

Q. If you were told that the only way to change the world for the better was to allow yourself to have as much money as you can spend, would you let yourself be rich?

"Laziness works. And the simple way to incorporate its health benefits into your life is simply to take a nap."

Tom Hodgkinson

Repeat your intention out loud. Write your intention in your journal, watch your words form, and see the magic here.

Around this time on any thirty-day change program, we can become sidetracked—so check in with yourself.

Are you still resonating with your intention? Are you enjoying the process? Are more resistances popping up in your life surrounding the intention? Are you seeing anything new about yourself?

This is a good time for a simple inquiry in order to breathe out any tightness and to re-establish this as a priority for you.

It is important to connect with your spirit.

You are pushing your brain out of the comfort zone so take this into account before you throw in the towel.

Claiming a few minutes in the morning before getting up—and in the evening before you go to sleep—to feel into your physical body and relax is so important. The stresses of even a "normal" day/week/month will build and make it more difficult over time to properly relax your body.

I know that my own stress levels can rise dramatically, and I can be unconscious of it except to feel more irritated throughout my day than usual. When I remember to let myself sink and be soft more regularly, life becomes better.

Today I would like you to give yourself something special—a small gift, some time out, a little pampering or half an hour in nature.

Notice when you feel the relief and repeat your intention in the present tense " I AM…."

A Wonderful Abundance of Water

Oh, the water in this world!

I see an abundance of water on Earth. There are puddles, streams,
Rivers, and oceans of wonderful water across this warm and wet planet.

Water that sustains life in so many ways. It gives birth to creatures of all shapes and sizes.

OH, the colours of water. The freshness of water!

I turn on taps and water pours abundantly into my cup.

My glass and bowl overflow with crystal clear, life-affirming water.

I allow it to slip down my throat in rivulets of energy.

I am prosperous in water. There is water everywhere.
Water falls from the sky and drips from the leaves on the trees.

I feel water in the air around me.

My body is made mostly of water.

I am a personal, wealthy, microcosmic planet of water.

I can share my water. I can make tea from my water.
I cleanse and renew myself with water every day!

I can splash like a dolphin in big ponds of clear, water.

This world is abundant IN WATER.

Water flows beneath our feet through the great Earth; it collects in pools for us to drink.

An abundance of water trickles through our fingers and over our grateful upturned faces.

When we wake up, we trust there is enough water.

People get together around water, animals congregate at water,
water is our collective commonality.

I love water. I am prosperous in water. I AM RICH in water!

Journal Your Thoughts

Q. Do you know anyone who seems truly abundant? Describe that life and note your emotional reaction.

"You can discover more about a person in an hour of play than in a year of conversation."

Plato

Day Eight

Repeat your intention out loud. Write your intention in your journal, watch your words form, and see the magic here.

When we are on the journey of deliberate creation, it is good to have an open dialogue with ourselves.

Shying away from our own fears can get in the way of the positive momentum necessary to reach our goals and manifest our desires.

Honesty about why we do what we do is imperative to finding and feeling motivation for change.

Today, contemplate *why* you would like this intention to come true.

What is it that you fear about staying the same?

Have a good look at your motivation for the intention you have set.

In truth there are no right or wrong motivating factors, but you do need to review your motivation in order to see whether it feels wrong or right to you personally.

Training yourself to feel a glitch between your intention and a belief system you hold is a powerful and effective tool for positive change.

For example, if you would like more money and have been intending for more money and then you take a look at your motivations, you might see your reasons for wanting more are along the vibration of 'I don't have enough' rather than 'I love the feeling of lots of money'—or 'I want to help others'—which may hide an agenda of superiority or be a distraction from your own sadness.

Knowing that the mind grows in neural clusters according to focus and that like thoughts attract like thoughts, we start to see that a vibrational or emotional shift is necessary in order to begin noticing really positive results.

Understanding the motivators can alert us to an underlying vibration that needs to be addressed.

This isn't to say there is anything wrong with wanting what you want at all; but it is important to clear the way and raise your own awareness levels.

If you notice a glitch, allow yourself to see, feel and understand. Let yourself know that although this vibration has been comfortable and has served you in the past you are now on a new journey.

Now that you have seen it, it won't feel so comfortable anymore.

Soothe yourself with good feeling words. Dialogue with yourself, remind yourself that anything is possible, and you are enjoying this new game of seeing wealth and health and joy all around you.

Deliberately changing a belief system takes focus and clarity. So be true to yourself. Listen to your fears, acknowledge them, feel them—and set them aside.

Feel The Flow

Oh, how weirdly satisfying this life can be: synchronistic and serendipitous.

Every morning the sun rises in a sweet, golden apex moment.

It makes us smile, day after day, apex moment after apex moment.

Little steps of sweet success,
small moments of appreciation.

Precious pearls of priceless experience, coming together
collecting like raindrops.

Necklaces of fairy magic looping and dancing
providing endless fascination.

Mesmerised by joy and excitement!

Each joyous moment expanding into another,
never tiring, filling with energy.

We are opening to the glories this universe has to offer.

I am so grateful, thankful, and appreciative of this opportunity to be alive—
to deliberately create a golden path of abundance, opening wider and brighter before me.

Love fills this path, gold surrounds us, we share in wealth and riches beyond compare!

Our dreams are coming true. We are guided and loved completely
in more beautiful ways than we could have ever imagined.

New connections, old connections, exciting opportunities!

A world of wealth.

The experience of money.

Financial abundance unlimited!

Journal Your Thoughts

Q. Why would you like to have lots of money?

"All that is important comes in quietness and waiting."

Patrick Lindsay

Day Nine

Repeat your intention out loud. Write your intention in your journal, watch your words form, and see the magic here.

You can be very proud of yourself for staying on track during this 30-day process.

Part of learning we have the potential to forge our own specific path in life is realising we have been doing it all along.

The difference now is that we can be deliberate about it. Focus and creation are not new to us as humans and spiritual beings; we are made this way. It was in the forgetting that things became difficult.

This is an awesome realisation because it shows the creative power is intact and strong—and we are not only capable of creating the life we dream of, but that we have been creating our dream all along.

To become a conscious and deliberate creator of well-being and abundance in your life, it is important to understand that the power of change is centred in the way we see ourselves. We are each responsible for our perception and responding emotional and energetic vibration that stems from this perception—no one can change that for us, no one else has that power.

It is true, that many of us have been influenced by intense, painful, and damaging experiences throughout life. We have been convinced that others hold the power, we have forgotten our own power and our inherent and natural capability of focusing and directing our energy. This results in feeling weak and small and easily pushed around by those who have lost sight of their own true power and use hurting others to reaffirm themselves. Even so, we are STRONG, or we wouldn't have survived. *Changing a dominant belief system of 'weak and small' is absolutely possible* and can be done moment by moment with awareness and self-forgiveness.

This is not an easy admittance, and many are not ready to see it this way.

Once we see this for what it is though, the possibilities for purposeful life creation become endless.

As you move through your day notice the experiences, whatever they might be, and say to yourself, 'I did this.'

Feel the feelings that arise—the positive and the negative—and find and revel in a feeling of personal power.

Billions of Excellent Eyes

Oh, eyes, beautiful glistening jewels of the human face.
They are everywhere—gorgeous expressive eyes, an abundance of eyes.

I am aware of the love in the eyes I see.

I note the varied colours: the green's, the chocolates, the blues, the golden, the ebony eyes.

I see the shiny hazel eyes and the sapphire eyes sparkling lovingly in my day.

There is a world of prosperous colour and energy flowing from eyes all over the earth.

I have adoration and appreciation for my own sweet eyes and all they see.

I allow my eyes to rest gently on this abundant world.
This is our community, where there is enough energy for everyone,
gathered in eyes and prosperously share with each other!

Eyes are the windows to our soul, we are abundant.

I am abundant in appreciation for the beauty I see in eyes all around me.

I awaken to eyes; I close my eyes and open to dreams.

I am grateful and fascinated by the rich wealth in the eye.

Journal Your Thoughts

Q. Do you think money is the root of all evil?

"Silence is the sleep that nourishes wisdom."
Francis Bacon

Day Ten

Repeat your intention out loud. Write your intention in your journal, watch your words form, and see the magic here.

Keep going on your self-love journey. Know in your heart that you are flowing with ease along the path of bringing your intention into physical reality.

Have faith that the steps you take are leading you exactly where you want to go.

You cannot predict all the details of your journey—but you can stay focused on the excitement as much as possible and the feelings you wish to experience when your manifestation is complete.

Remember—it is the feeling you are after, not the thing or the form you believe you have intended for.

The intention will make itself happen in response to your feelings. So, use your emotions as indicators. When you start feeling miserable, breathe out and imagine how you would prefer to feel—then work your way toward that feeling, little by little.

Also, it is helpful to note that a thought is a manifestation too; it is the first layer or blueprint.

As your positive feelings grow in response to the thought, this becomes like a layer bringing more substance to your dream.

The next noticeable density is the creative impulse that occurs—the heart-beating ideas and little, exciting inspirations that lead you to take certain actions.

These actions may not *seem* to directly affect the manifestation of your intention into a physically, substantial outcome—but don't assume you understand this part of the process.

Just keep finding your feet and enjoying the feelings, listening to the whispers, and following your inspiration—it all reveals itself over time.

List any ideas that occur for you, they don't need to be brought into reality straight away, but it helps enhance the energy to acknowledge them.

Feel The Flow

It's on the breeze, the sweet smell of success!

I can feel it, I can smell it, it's like the rising smell of cookies baking.

Even the feeling is a manifestation: the sensation, the touch,
the taste, is all a dream coming true.

The intention is for an awesome life, an open heart, abiding security and true freedom!

It's already here, so many wonderful things happening every day. I live in the receptive zone.

New ideas are forming easily—marketing tricks for pure success coming our way.

The sun rose, the sun set, books were sold, art created, food prepared,
people smiled; the air was fresh.

I am free, I am here, I am present.

Those around me are jumping with joy, birth is on the horizon.

People are noticing, people are connecting and wanting what I have.

Money is pouring into my bank account from all different sources.

Life is plush with abundance.

Air, food, love, money, energy, and happiness.

I am a winner.

I am happy.

I am vibrant, I am sexy, I am alive!

Journal Your Thoughts

Q. If you had an endless supply of money, how do you believe you would feel?

"Time out is a good thing.
You can shift to Paradise in the next breath and a sense of wellness
and timelessness will be the wonderful result."

Cheryl Melody

Day Eleven

Think of your intention with love. Don't harp on it anymore, as it is the letting go stage of the process now. From here on, when you bring your intention into focus, allow it to light up and fly away.

Have you even got an inkling of just how awesome you are yet?

You have within you the power to create worlds; every cell is driven by a nucleus of immense potential.

All you need to do is know your wishes have been addressed by the universe and are all on their way to you.

There are so many ways for the positive story of your life to come together pleasingly for you. But you must relax about it, breathe out and let it go.

Surrender the work to the universe or your higher self. Allow time for all the necessary components to come together to bring your dream into reality.

You have only one job and that is to expect and affirm that everything is always working out for you—for the highest good of all.

A Gratitude of Glorious Green

I open my eyes and look out the window—I am in a world abundant with GREEN.

Green the glorious aura of the heart, the translucent colour of emeralds and deep ocean
currents.

The wealth of green feeds me. I see leaves and grasses of different shades,
many different shapes and textures to absorb.

Life abounds in green, so much gorgeous green to share with all the beings of the Earth.

Abundance is green, money is green, some of the most nutritious food is green,
green is everywhere!

Waves of green flow through me, swirling around me,
gently soothing me and filling me with a generous feeling of wealth and wonder.

I feel protected and loved by the green in my world.

We can lay our blankets on soft green grass, enjoy our picnics by mossy green river rocks.

Green is life—abundant life. Green clothes, green shoes, green hats, green jelly.

I am rich with the colour green.

Journal Your Thoughts

Q. If I gave you $100 right now and said you had 60 seconds to spend it, what would you do?

"Work is not always required. There is such a thing as sacred idleness."

George MacDonald

Day Twelve

Think of your intention with love. Don't harp on it anymore, as it is the letting go stage of the process now. From here on, when you bring your intention into focus, allow it to light up and fly away.

There is nothing stopping you from being who you want to be except your self-perceived and self-perpetuated limitations.

Have you ever heard anything as delightful as that previous sentence?

Although life difficulties, injustices, and environmental factors influence our self-belief—deep down in the centre of your heart and soul, we remain whole and complete. Your true self has been unmarred. When you focus back here, on your own perfection and potential—there is nothing at all, whatsoever, in any way shape, or form that stands in the way of you being a healthy, happy, magnificently abundant person on Earth.

Nothing but a silly old belief system or two—and what is a belief anyway, but a thought you thought long enough for it to stick.

And now, because it's got a foothold in your brain, it has become easy to manifest experiences related to it.

But you know this now, you have an advantage!

So when something happens you do not enjoy, ask yourself—'How did I get here?' 'What is it about the way I thought that connects to this experience?'

The trick is to feel the feelings attached to the experience—and wonder how often you have had that feeling before, and why you feel you need to keep experiencing this feeling?

This personal inquiry brings beliefs into conscious awareness—highlighting them for what they are and allowing you to recognise them more easily as they come up. Eventually, you will have no need for them in your life ever again.

Feel The Flow

Success comes easily to me.

The softer I am, the more present I am, the easier everything is.

I don't need to work hard or try hard anymore.

All I do I can do easily, softly, joyfully.

When I breathe out, all my worries are released and dissolved
and I am filled with inspiration.

I look forward to the shimmering beauty of each day, the newness
the possibilities and the satisfaction of my financial success.

My work moves like the tide, consistently appreciated,
easily seen, people are thrilled and inspired by my creations.

I feel wealthier in spirit and my spirit shines because of this new love I feel for myself.

Those I love are enjoying the spin-off of the abundant life I am manifesting now.

Life is good.

Money comes easily to me in unexpected, delightful ways,
more money than I can spend is flowing to me now.

I am rich!
I am happy!
I am free!

Journal Your Thoughts

Q. Do You believe there is a limit to the money it is possible for you to receive?

"Sometimes the most important thing in a whole day
is the rest we take between two deep breaths."

Etty Hillesum

Day Thirteen

Think of your intention with love. Don't harp on it anymore, as it is the letting go stage of the process now. From here on, when you bring your intention into focus, allow it to light up and fly away.

Do you judge yourself or others very often? Judgement can keep us stuck in old patterns of belief, but they are also excellent indicators *of our own beliefs.*

Notice the thoughts that come to your mind today. Are they kind or are they cynical? Are your judgements optimistic?

It is interesting to hear ourselves comment on life. Becoming a witness to our judgements can provide us the detachment necessary for a rational evaluation of our own circumstances.

If we remember that judgement is a completely subjective experience, we can begin sorting the wheat from the chaff in our belief system.

We judge a certain way because we are programmed to judge things that way—not because it is who we really are or what we really think.

If we want to clear the path for our consciously created life to unfold—we would do well to relax our judgements and understand that everything in the world has only the meaning that we, personally, give it.

Underneath our interpretation and judgement, it simply IS and that is all there is to it.

An Abundance of BUGS!

Oh, this marvelous earth abundant with tiny creatures!

Little bugs that keep our ecosystem running perfectly.

We are supported by healthy, vibrant bugs that run around fixing everything.

Little happy helpful bugs in our body, little bugs cleaning up our waterways.

Life is prosperous with positive little bugs.

Butterflies, dragonflies, caterpillars and more,
little bugs that eat our rubbish and clean up our wealthy world!

We are ABUNDANT with bugs, there are countless bugs necessary to our Earth's continued evolution.

Bugs for everyone to share!

Journal Your Thoughts

Q. A belief is just a thought we have thought often enough for it to stick. If there was one belief about money you would like to change, what would it be?

"There must be quite a few things that a hot bath won't cure, but I don't know many of them."

Sylvia Plath

Day Fourteen

Think of your intention with love now. You don't need to create it over and over again, as it is the letting go stage of the process. From here on, when you bring your intention into focus allow it to light up and fly away.

Everything comes back to your emotions and to you—consciously embracing your role as the commander of your emotional ship.

Deciding to have input into the creation of your personal journey is the same as making the choice to view your life from an empowered perspective.

One way to take the emotional bull by the horns is to find time and courage to sit with your bull and get to know him.

Gaining awareness of who you are and what makes you react emotionally is the key to directing your world with ease and grace and resulting in positive, palpable results.

Be the captain; watch your emotions as though they are your crew.

Notice as you find your inner world changing. Be aware of the way feelings lead you to want to say or do something.

Notice and breathe. Notice and stop. Take a second before you react.

This is good training and will help you to recognise your less than loving thoughts, understand yourself and change your reactions if necessary.

Unacknowledged emotions can stand in the way of your dreams coming true—but being willing to relax into your emotions and see them clearly is the ticket to success.

Activity: List your successes

List every little success and do it as often as you can remember. A success is a good feeling moment. For example, the cute boy at the checkout smiled at me; the cake I baked was delicious; I sold an artwork; I met a new friend; I found a dollar; I won a competition. Don't be afraid to put in a few dreams as well. Remember the brain isn't differentiating between reality and dream—it is the vibration we are shifting!

My bath was relaxing; the garden looks great; I found the perfect shoes; I love my friends; I have more money than I can possibly spend!

This is where you can get caught up in rational need to justify your dreams. Just notice this and remind yourself that the universe is a huge and mysterious place. There are myriad ways for you to deliver on your dreams that you don't know about with your little bitty brain!

Affirmation

Everything is turning out more exquisitely than I believe, even if I don't believe it yet!

Repeat Out Loud

I am a powerful soul. I am being guided and supported at all times.

I know the right decisions to make.

I walk confidently toward my dreams.

I am living my dreams in so many ways already.

My work in the world is desired, admired, acquired.

I am creating a silvery sparkly network of switched-on peers and benefactors.

My money is following, and my abundance is expanding rapidly.

There is more love, money, and connection for me than I can imagine.

Prosperity thinking is all so easy now!

I am appreciated and deeply loved.

I have a powerful imagination that can focus and create marvelous things.

Money flows into my bank account; more money than I can spend.

I appreciate the financial flow.

I'm a success, a winner, a wonder!

My body is strong, supple, and healthy.

My family and friends are happy, connected, and enthusiastic.

My lover is sensual, powerful, and energetic.

I open to all the universe offers me.

Q. Where does money come from? Who invented it? Contemplate the history of money.

"How much time do you spend in the World of Yes?"
SARK

Day Fifteen

Think of your intention with love now. You don't need to create it over and over again, as it is the letting go stage of the process. From here on, when you bring your intention into focus allow it to light up and fly away.

Every moment is an opportunity to remind yourself of how well you are doing.

You are on the path to a kind of well-being that not many people are experiencing.

Caught up in a stress-driven world where we are constantly competing for a sense of self-worth and working hard to get where we think we need to go; it is easy to miss the imperative signs that lead us to peace.

The difference between living like that and living as a self-actualised being is that those signs become blatantly obvious when you take the time to love and appreciate yourself.

Focus on your sense of connection to the air you breathe. Take a moment to visualise a clear running stream, sink into the vision and become the stream.

When you know you are connected to all that is, and learn that your energy affects all things, it is the next logical choice to raise your awareness—and in turn, your vibration, making everything just that little bit sweeter. In fact, being a mathematical universe, it naturally and logically raises the vibration for you.

When you become aware, the vibration shifts to something much more sparkly and revealing.

You are now tuned to serendipity and the acknowledgement of serendipity leads to more serendipity.

In truth, YOU become an abundant universe!

A Flush of Fabulous Fabric

Fabric! Cloth of all kinds, I am abundant in this beautiful creation.

A plethora of patterns to thrill us all: floral, geometric, swirls and polka-dots!

There is a wealth of scintillating, stimulating, serendipitous material all over the world.
We are prosperous in FABRIC!

How fortunate we are—how creative the human mind, producing a richness of texture
and hue to cover our bodies and decorate our floors!

How abundant is this earth with beings that love to dance and flaunt gorgeous cloth.

Ballerinas in tutus and little people in bright colours. Kings and queens in golden royal dress!

We are a fandango of extraordinary prosperity, fabric that hugs our delicious form
and plays in shadows and light.

I feel so lucky to be a part of this fabricious weave of wonder!

Journal your thoughts

Q. Do you enjoy the sunshine? Golden abundant sunshine. What do you love about the sunshine?

"The paradox of relaxation is the renewal of mind,
rekindling of spirit and revitalising of strength."

Lailah Gifty Akita

Day Sixteen

Think of your intention with love now. You don't need to create it over and over again, as it is the letting go stage of the process. From here on, when you bring your intention into focus allow it to light up and fly away.

The truth is, it doesn't matter what you are doing. It is how you address your experience that is important.

If you are doing a menial job for a small amount of money and you wish you were somewhere else, do your best to use the situation as an opportunity for the practice of presence. You don't get somewhere more satisfying by complaining, feeling terrible, or projecting outside of your present experience.

Dreaming big and escaping your present are two opposing forces.

What we resist persists, as they say. Just like a cut on your foot that you ignore until it becomes infected, so is it with the emotions of dissatisfaction and disappointment.

The grumpy, dissatisfied vibration might be what got you here in the first place.

Our bodies are made for sensing and processing. If we impede the processing function by stopping the dial at discontent, we won't reach a better feeling place—not on any real and permanent level anyway!

Try something different with your emotions.

Try finding the positive aspects of what you do even if it is packaging rubber washing up gloves!

Think of the gratitude someone who washes up in really hot water every day for a living might feel as they slip into the gloves you are making.

See your part in the whole.

Congratulate yourself for being of service.

Developing and maintaining a vibration of acceptance and appreciation will lead you to a far better feeling place and give you clarity of choice.

With this new perspective you will see the opportunities for change begin to appear in your life **as inspired thought and action.**

Feel The Flow

There is a warmth trickling through me
an abundant sensation of love.

Life is intriguing fascinating and mysterious.

Unseen help is all around me. I am wealthy and awakened.

I embrace the universal treasures that are my birthright.
I am a child of the abundant Goddess,
the receiver of all good things.

Life is always working out for me—the more I notice the stronger it gets!

I am excited at the indications of success all around me.

My connections with others are deepening and my connection with myself is strengthening.

As a result, I am seeing regular financial inflow.

I feel easy about creating wealth.
I believe I am a success.

My life increases in positivity and financial abundance daily.

I am a winner!

This life is a big win of love, large sums of money, and worldly appreciation and recognition.

I see money flowing into my pocket every day while I am sleeping, eating, singing, and
bathing.

I am happy to be of service.
I am happy to receive!

Journal Your Thoughts

Q. Are you a generous person? What does generosity feel like?

"By having a clear vision, even a short vision of what will happen in the future.
We will be less worried and feel a little bit confident, and calm because
we can manage our life in the world that is changing every second."

Ly Nguyen

Think of your intention with love now. You don't need to create it over and over again, as it is the letting go stage of the process. From here on, when you bring your intention into focus allow it to light up and fly away.

The hard truth is that, although it feels nice to have someone say or do something uplifting, it is not the key to developing your own personal power. Yes, it helps to surround yourself with kind and loving people—and just the fact you can surround yourself like this means you are doing well in your vibrational world.

If you perceive the external world as unkind, unsafe, and unfair—this is the measure of where your vibration is currently tuned.

Don't panic, we all have these days. But do stop and feel around for a more positive vibration— and play at encouraging yourself in that direction.

There is no doubt we are one—and we affect each other—but the effect we have is not in truth due to the circumstance. It comes down to our *perception of the* circumstance.

Another person may perceive a situation that has brought you to your knees in emotional distress and feel no emotional response to it at all.

Each experience is 100% our own to work with, play with, and feel our way through.

When we get a handle on this idea, we find ourselves in a whole new world where energy can be explored safely and emotions can be recognised, tamed, and followed.

Practicing uplifting ourselves is paramount to growing the neuron sets in our brain that support the manifesting of our conscious intentions.

Spend a moment revisiting your intention and feel the way it resonates within you.

While thinking, soften yourself and soothe yourself into a state of being that requires no outcome at all.

Try just enjoying the idea of your intention—and the feeling you can imagine it provoking— whether it ever comes to be or not.

When you can manage this, you are winning big time!

A River of Kindness

Every time I turn on my computer, I see beautiful, heart-warming stories of kindness.

I wake up to an abundance of kindness in my life and in this world.

I see a never-ending supply of kindness.

Kindness can be a simple smile or gesture.
I notice it all the time in others—and from deep within.
I feel the urge to be kind.

I am wealthy in Kindness. I can give it away with joy and ease.

There are so many opportunities to experience kindness.

Even when I feel not so good, I only need to remember a moment of kindness
and I can start a roll of good feeling thoughts.

Kindness is natural to me and to the people in my life.
Human beings thrive on kindness. Kindness is as abundant as oxygen.

We are a prosperous, kind collective of wonderful creators.

Journal Your Thoughts

Q. Do you associate winning with money? Are you a competitive person?

"Relaxation means releasing all concern and tension and letting
the natural order of life flow through one's being."

Donald Curtis

Day Eighteen

Think of your intention with love now. You don't need to create it over and over again, as it is the letting go stage of the process. From here on, when you bring your intention into focus allow it to light up and fly away.

It is very easy to throw a bit of a tantrum on the road to improved well-being—especially if you are being asked to give up your old habits of blame and self-pity.

This is where having a little bit of faith that there is something more outside our comfort zones come in handy.

There is something valuable and powerful that we don't have much memory of as yet—but, if we can keep breathing and letting go, being willing to allow the mystery to unfold, we will be shown the way step-by-step.

Our true selves will emerge, and our souls will celebrate with newfound purpose.

There is nothing to do, nothing to seek—we are already exactly where we are meant to be on our path. We only need to calm ourselves enough to recognise and accept our position.

It is from this point we send out the message for our abundant universe to hear and respond to.

In effect, we are letting go of the reins and handing our concerns over to a force that is connected at the very core of who we are—and knows exactly what to do next.

Your job is to catch yourself as you are gearing up for a moment of resistance and make this connection a conscious one.

Even as you feel the discomfort, know that what is happening is that you are forgetting again. This is your indication to breathe out and remember.

Appreciate your awareness and congratulate your awesome self for remembering and coming back into alignment with your dreams.

Feel The Flow

I can feel energy vibrating in my body.

I am awake.

I am in touch.

My skin is soft to touch. The breath feels good as it enters me. I am abundant in oxygen.

I am flushed and rich with life.

Everywhere I look things take on a shine.
This is a golden life: simple, easy, successful.

I turn away from old ideas and create new neural pathways in my beautiful brain—
pathways that support a sense of wealth and security.

I feel safe and satisfied.

I am feeling so excited and enthusiastic about life.

I see evidence of my new abundant paradigm everywhere I look.

Every day, new evidence of my success and wealth are appearing before my eyes.
.
Money, energy, and life force flow easily and joyfully through me.

I attract good things!

Journal Your Thoughts

Q. Do you believe that being poor means you are a better person than someone with a lot of money?

"When was the last time you spent a quiet moment just doing nothing - just sitting and looking at the sea, or watching the wind blowing the tree limbs, or waves rippling on a pond, a flickering candle or children playing in the park?"

Ralph Marston

Day Nineteen

Think of your intention with love now. You don't need to create it over and over again, as it is the letting go stage of the process. From here on, when you bring your intention into focus allow it to light up and fly away.

Remembering **now** is a like gold in the bank. The more you do it, the more you will remember to do it—and the better and better life will become.

Here and now is where the answers to all of your questions lie. Spend a few breaths completely present—and don't be surprised if you get an inspired idea!

It isn't always as easy as it sounds.

Sometimes there is what seems like pain or discomfort in the now—but I have found that this is still not *quite now.* If you can be strong and push your feet into the ground, holding your palms together, concentrating on the physical sensations of your emotions—your system will soon settle into the focus that *you* choose to take.

Practicing in the car is quite powerful and it helps to keep us safe. Holding our hands on the steering wheel—feeling the car's rumble—watching the road—all done with the simple, conscious intention to spend more time present.

Practice, practice, practice really does pay off.

A Wealth of Wild and Winsome Children

Children—soft beautiful children; an abundance of glorious innocence.

Little feet running and jumping, playing, and laughing. Squealing children, happy to be alive.

Prosperous with energy; tingling with joyous enthusiasm.

I am abundant in the opportunity to adore children;
to learn from the little ones with their wide, open, and abundant hearts.

This world has sweet children covering its magical surface. We are wealthy in children.

We have before us a generation of innovation—of brilliant creative potential.

We are so lucky. I am so wealthy—so rich in the experience of new life; delicious beginnings.

I experience the pure happiness of joyous human laughter.

I am awakening my own childlike faith.

I AM a loving, trusting, and abundant child.

Journal Your Thoughts

Q. Do you believe you deserve to have money?

"Sometimes it's important to work for that pot of gold. But other times it's essential to take time off and to make sure that your most important decision in the day simply consists of choosing."
Douglas Pagels

Think of your intention with love now. You don't need to create it over and over again, as it is the letting go stage of the process. From here on, when you bring your intention into focus allow it to light up and fly away.

We teach best what we most need to learn. In this respect, examining our lives for what we are trying to improve in others can be most revealing.

Write down your common complaints, and then make a personal inquiry.

'Do I follow my own rules?'

'Am I avoiding addressing this in myself?'

'Why do I value this so highly that I must harass someone else to change?'

'Do I prefer the idea of righteousness over happiness?'

It is worth being a bit of a taskmaster when using this method—because as you come to see more clearly the irrationality of most of your complaints, the more of your own lack of self-acceptance is released and the happier you (and everyone around you) can be.

Feel The Flow

Abundance flows!

I see clearly the value of the people in my life.

I hear them laugh.

I see them expand.

Other's success is my success.

Where I once felt envy or competition, I now understand that the more I see success in the people around me, the more I am attracting success and abundance into my own life!

The flow of love and excitement that fills others hearts is my own excitement.

I am inspired by the ideas and success others bring to the table.

I am seeing with clarity and purpose.

I am looking forward with jubilant anticipation to hearing my friends next success stories.

Journal Your Thoughts

Q. Does Money equal hard work for you?

"Every great dream begins with a dreamer. Always remember, you have within you the strength, the patience, and the passion to reach for the stars to change the world."

Harriet Tubman

Day Twenty-one

Think of your intention with love now. You don't need to create it over and over again, as it is the letting go stage of the process. From here on, when you bring your intention into focus allow it to light up and fly away.

If you were the last person on Earth, would you take the time to fall in love? If there were no one to impress and no one to compare yourself with, would you be able to be happy?

You are the only one here and the way you view yourself is *exactly* what you will transmit energetically to the world around you.

The more consistently you love yourself, the more consistently you will notice love in your external world. The way your world looks is in exact response to how much you truly love, respect, accept and approve of yourself.

Being present—and being kind to yourself and making your emotions your gauge—will lead you into the sweet spot of self-love.

The deeper you allow yourself to fall into the wondrousness of who you are the stronger you will perceive your connection with the entire universal consciousness and no longer will you believe in the limitation of resources.

You will have access to boundless love—and love is literally the fuel that drives it all.

Love is life. Life is universal energy. Universal energy is abundance of all things—including money, and enthusiasm.

Smiles

How deep is a smile?

A smile is so deep it transforms the face.

I am abundant in the ability to smile—and in the sensational ability to perceive a smile.

I am rich with an awareness of smiles.

My heart is touched every time I see a smile,
it is as though your soul has reached in with loving fingers and stroked my inner being.

Prosperity is apparent in another's smile—smiling feels so good.

Smiling is wonderful to bathe in.

I bathe in smiles everyday.

Smiles are free and everywhere—for all to share.

I give you my smile and I receive yours and if you don't smile at me,
I don't mind because I know someone else will!

A smile is the first step to health,
it has a physical impact of intense positivity on the body.

Our smiling mechanism is a magic button that brings love to all.

We are a world abundant in the most valuable commodity—smiles.

Sometimes we might need to dig for a smile but once it is found it quickly multiplies.

OH, how wealthy we are.

I appreciate this never ending, limitless, abundant supply of smile!

Journal Your Thoughts

Q. Do you believe in a vibrational universe? Where the external experiences matches your internal vibration/belief system?

"Live your truth. Express your love. Share your enthusiasm. Take action towards your dreams.
Walk your talk. Dance and sing to your music. Embrace your blessings.
Make today worth remembering."

Steve Maraboli

Day Twenty-two

Think of your intention with love now. You don't need to create it over and over again, as it is the letting go stage of the process. From here on, when you bring your intention into focus allow it to light up and fly away.

You are only experiencing this body because of every breath you take. These breaths can count for so much more than we give them credit for. Each breath is like a tiny life—and for many bacteria in our body, it is as literal as that.

One breath equals one life. Notice the way you breathe. Are you breathing through your mouth or your nose? Are your breaths deep and life giving or are they short and shallow? Your lungs are wanting to be used to their full capacity your body needs the oxygen from your breathe to make it all the way around you—down to the tips of your fingers and the tips of your toes.

Without good levels of oxygen in your blood, we can produce too much of the hormone Cortisol. We need Cortisol. It serves many important functions in your body—like supporting immunity and regulating blood sugar levels—but it is also produced as part of the fight/flight mechanism.

So basically, stress causes a rise in Cortisol—and in turn too much of it causes us to respond as though we are in danger. We need to calm ourselves and learn to breathe deeply and slowly in order to stop this panic cycle, which has disastrous physical results—including weight gain and heart problems.

There is a reason hospitals monitor oxygen and increase our intake levels of it when we are sick. It is literally of the highest healing potential. The good news is we can deliver this easily to ourselves. Breathing is essential and needs to be respected. We share the air with all around us—imagine it filled with sparkling components that bring well-being to your world.

Spend some time with yourself taking into account your breathing patterns. Watch them, smile at them, and marvel at our physical machine.

Feel The Flow

I see a coin on the ground and realise that every sparkle in this universe is like a smile
from the heart of all that is.

I will never want because I am connected to this beautiful world.

All I need to do is ask.

If I was hungry, someone would feed me.
If someone asked me for food, I would feed them.

I am flooded with a sense of prosperity and abundance.
I cannot control the pouring into me of all good things.

Now I have let the gates fall open the universe is unstoppable.

My heart has opened and I am receiving inspiration to give, to be of service—
to receive what I need and more.

I feel connected and secure and full to the overflowing with an abundance of LOVE!

Journal Your Thoughts

Q. Imagine if every time you took a breath it translated to $1 in the bank! But every time you took a deep conscious breath it equaled $50!

"If I cannot do great things, I can do small things in a great way."

Martin Luther King Jr.

Day Twenty-three

Think of your intention with love now. You don't need to create it over and over again, as it is the letting go stage of the process. From here on, when you bring your intention into focus allow it to light up and fly away.

Take a look around your house—is it tidy or messy; dirty or clean?

What are your cupboards and drawers like—cluttered or organised?

What does your house say about you?

And more importantly, as you look around now—how does it make you *feel*?

The external world can be seen as a reflection of your psyche. Look at your computer screen for example—is it jam-packed with apps and icons? Are things you want difficult—or easy—to find? If it was de-cluttered, would you feel better?

What does an organised shelf in your kitchen feel like, as opposed to a cluttered shelf? Look around your life and note the feelings each corner or aspect of it brings. Simply put, does your lifestyle trigger stress—or does it make you feel comforted and calm?

Self-awareness is KEY to finding what feels good—and consequently staying in the soft receptive zone, where opportunities are clear to see and life options are easier to follow.

Get accustomed to feeling your way around your world.

Check-in with these feelings, because they hold a clue to the pressure and expectation you put on yourself.

Do you value organisation or do you value freedom and flow? Why do you value what you value? Can you see where you naturally strike a satisfactory balance between your values?

Is your new intention for well-being in alignment with these values you hold? Can you adjust your values a little here and a little there until you feel easy about them?

You don't want to be hung up on a particular way of being if it conflicts with your desire for well-being and abundance. So, bring it all into your awareness and let some go.

The values we hold are only thoughts that have protected and supported us at one stage in our lives. Maybe we felt we could control something, and that gave us a sense of ease.

It doesn't mean it is right for us now. It can be absolutely appropriate to thank our value system for its good work and set about adjusting our habits to suit new dreams.

A Delightful Abundance of Technology

My fingers tick and click on the soft yet potent buttons of technology!

We have technology all around us—supporting us, connecting us, and inspiring us.

We are wealthy in beautiful, intelligent, and technological people—
with innovative ideas to make life stimulating and exciting.

Technology at every turn—a virtual, fascinating, sci-fi adventure!

I love the sense of 'anything is possible' that the technological era offers me.

I feel as though the world is at my fingertips.

I enjoy the momentum forward, the futuristic possibilities—
the wealth of information I have access to due to the awesome experience of technology.

I am grateful for all the connections and communication
that the digital world of technology offers me.

Journal Your Thoughts

Q. Can you feel the energy that cushions your heart? Is it light or heavy? Stay with it for a while, let it speak to you.

"To laugh often and love much; to win the respect of intelligent persons and the affection of children; to earn the approbation of honest citizens and endure the betrayal of false friends; to appreciate beauty; to find the best in others; to give of one's self; to leave the world a bit better, whether by a healthy child, a garden patch or a redeemed social condition; to have played and laughed with enthusiasm and sung with exultation; to know even one life has breathed easier because you have lived — this is to have succeeded."

Bessie Anderson Stanley

Day Twenty-four

Think of your intention with love now. You don't need to create it over and over again, as it is the letting go stage of the process. From here on, when you bring your intention into focus allow it to light up and fly away.

A great trick for encouraging a new perspective is locating the positive in every situation—even the terrible ones.

Start by practicing with small things, like stubbing your toe. ''Well, that's reminding me to be more present and conscious of where my feet are!'

Stubbing the toes—or minor stings and burns—are also great ways to practice 'feeling the pain.' These are pains you know will go away—they are intense and easy to track.

And as a bonus, if you can allow yourself to sink into the pain of a stubbed toe or burn, you will find that the body responds by quieting down it's pain receptors. It is as if it knows you are aware of it and doesn't need to scream at you any longer.

Feeling your emotional pain is much the same as feeling a physical pain—just sometimes subtler.

You can be sensitive enough to locate an emotional hurt in your body and stay with it until it unwinds.

Practicing looking on the bright side of life is—like most things—easier when you've diligently done it for a while.

Notice your resistance to taking responsibility in this way—and smile and do it anyway. This is a fast-track to more consistent well-being—which in turns opens the flood gates for the physical manifestation of your desires.

Feel The Flow

Like paint runs onto the canvas or water flows generously down the stream,
so does the abundant flow of the universe course through my veins.

This is a vibrational universe.

I only need to imagine the energy flowing with ease and grace—and so it is.

I am powerfully effective in bringing prosperity into focus.

Gold, silver, love, water—I am a receptive and easy being to all good things.
I know how to find what feels good for me.

I let myself experience soft allowing.

Soft allowing is who I really am.

Journal Your Thoughts

Q. What motivates you to get what you want? List all the words and thoughts that come to mind.

"A wo/man is not called wise because s/he talks and talks again; but if s/he is peaceful, loving and fearless then s/he is in truth called wise."

Buddha

Think of your intention with love now. You don't need to create it over and over again, as it is the letting go stage of the process. From here on, when you bring your intention into focus allow it to light up and fly away.

What brings you joy?

This is a question that begs an answer—especially in a world where the options for enjoying life are huge.

Take a gratitude check. Are you appreciating your life? Are you loving the things and the people you already have—or are you letting what you don't have dominate your emotional experience?

If you are allowing the lack to permeate, then you have a lot of joy you are not tapping into. Make a list of the things that you like and see how it feels to read through it.

When you encounter a raw feeling of lack, feel it in your body and let it go. Say 'I am willing to release and change'—then focus back on your 'like list.'

Change the words in your 'like list' around until it feels good and easy when you read it.

This is one way to reinvigorate your joy and then milk that joy for all you can.

Pepper your day with moments of joy until they blend together and become who and what you are on Earth.

This is a sure-fire way to creating a life you desire. Especially when you consider that whatever intention you have made is more about the feeling you believe it will bring you.

If you can engender that feeling within you now—before you can physically see the thing you want—you are funneling power into your intention and literally bringing it to life.

A Bounty of Beautiful Birds

I hear birdsong as I awaken each day, an orchestra of celebration—
dozens of harmonious voices coming together to welcome the light.

Pretty little birds in an abundance of colour—
feathers flickering in the sky, a rainbow of creation.

This earth is home to over ten thousand species of birds—
flying birds, floating birds, walking birds, and running birds.

So many birds we can hardly count—a rich, fascinating abundance of birds.

Birds that talk, birds that hum, and birds that love.

When we look, we see birds—like angels, observing, communicating and vibrating
prosperity, health, and happiness.

Journal Your Thoughts

Q. Do you feel ready to take responsibility for your financial well-being?

"Gratitude helps you to grow and expand; gratitude brings joy and laughter
into your life and into the lives of all those around you."

Eileen Caddy

Day Twenty-six

Think of your intention with love now. You don't need to create it repeatedly, as it is the letting go stage of the process. From here on, when you bring your intention into focus allow it to light up and fly away.

You hear a lot of people say, "I feel I don't deserve…."—whether it's success, happiness, or just for things to just go smoothly.

There is an undercurrent of 'I'm not worthy' buzzing in our society. Where does this come from? Why do such beautiful, powerful co-creators get the idea they are not worthy of living the life they wish for?

You can probably trace it back to values that circle around 'greed' and 'guilt' for asking. We are told NO a lot when we are little—we are asked to give, in order to get. To do our work for money, our homework for praise—be quieter, be smaller, be better—and so on. Rarely do we hear adults say to children, 'you're here to have fun—just love yourself. If you don't feel like doing it, don't do it—do something that feels better.'

While all this is normal—and serves us in some ways—it is not our natural state of being. It doesn't encourage us to know how powerful and wonderful we are.

As we grow up into these cloaked versions of ourselves, it becomes difficult for us to truly respect ourselves. One thing that properly deserves respect is integrity. Most of us are floundering a bit under the weight of other people's expectations and haven't found our personal integrity—the grit needed to get up and say THIS IS ME.

Once we start becoming aware of ourselves and understanding our need for self-love, we begin to see how great we are. We then feel more confident about being ourselves and in this we gain our OWN respect.

Play with the feelings of worthiness—give yourself a little talking to. Let *you* know that it is time to see the truth and to stand up and be okay with accepting the love and honour that the universe wishes to give you.

Accept the gift and see that you absolutely do deserve the respect you can now give to yourself.

Feel The Flow

Sometimes I feel a tingling in my fingertips and if I get very quiet...
I realise they are dancing to the music of the universe.

My rhythm has taken to this soft melody and is finding its way to enter the world.

I am a creative abundant, fully realised being.
I deserve this prosperous lifestyle.

My soul is buoyant, and I feel appreciation spiraling out from my heart,
in rainbow colours on waves of love.

I feel abundant because I AM Abundant

I am gifted with a physical/spiritual existence that brings joy after joy after joy.

Journal Your Thoughts

Q. Do you think if you took a little time to meditate on a sense of joy and abundance each day that you would start to shift your perspective?

"Act happy, Feel happy, Be happy, Without a Reason in the World.
Then you can love and do what you will."

Dan Millman

Day Twenty-seven

Think of your intention with love now. You don't need to create it repeatedly, as it is the letting go stage of the process. From here on, when you bring your intention into focus allow it to light up and fly away.

To consciously receive the power of the universe and use it deliberately to create our desired life, we must acknowledge our personal connection to it.

The fact is we are already creating all the time. It isn't about learning how to create—you can't help but do it. It is about saying *yes* to connection—about encouraging our brain to stay focused on YES.

Being anchored in the now is a powerful technique perceived by the universe—or your higher, more aligned self as a YES. One way to monitor your sense of connection to your source/intuition is through your inter-personal intelligence levels—or your ability to cope in certain situations relating to an external object.

This includes relating to people, animals, situations, food, and so on. Ask yourself, 'how does it feel to look people in the eye when I am talking to them?'

'Am I actually listening to what this person is saying and am I feeling the feelings in my body that their words are triggering?'

How do you feel when you walk into a room full of people?

Notice the way your body or 'emotional detector' responds in different circumstances. How do you feel when you are standing in front of certain foods—is your body saying *yes* or *no*?'

Are your feelings or thoughts getting more airplay in your day?

Slow down a bit and try allowing your feelings to lead you, feel before you respond, give yourself a breath or two.

When you are doing this, you are meditating on the present moment and what it is offering you. You are in direct connection with your source.

When you feel soft, easy, calm, good, excited, and natural—then it is a yes. You are in alignment with your inner voice—and it is a great time to take inspired action. If it is hard, uneasy, painful, uncomfortable, confusing, and so on—it is not time to act. Wait until you have come back into alignment. Take time to privately address the reaction in your body before responding.

Make this a habit and soon you will be naturally walking into awesome opportunities and the exact circumstances to bring your intentions into manifestation.

Suggestion

Visualisation is a fun and effective tool to bridge the perceived gap between us and *All That Is*.

Make visualisation part of your morning practice to relax your body. Visualise yourself dissolving into the air around you.

With every breath, let go and allow yourself to merge and blend. When you feel ready, breathe yourself back into form and with a smile—and get up and start your day.

Feel The Flow

I am appreciated and deeply loved.

I have a powerful imagination that can focus and create marvellous things.

Money flows into my bank account—more money than I can spend.

I appreciate the financial flow.

I'm a success, a winner, a wonder!

My body is strong, supple, and healthy.

My family and friends are happy, connected, and enthusiastic.

My lover is sensual, powerful, and energetic.

I open to all the universe offers me.

Journal Your Thoughts

Q. How willing are you to change?

"If you're having difficulty coming up with new ideas, then slow down.
For me, slowing down has been a tremendous source of creativity. It has allowed me
to open up - to know that there's life under the earth and that I have to let it come
through me in a new way. Creativity exists in the present moment.
You can't find it anywhere else."

Natalie Goldberg

Day Twenty-eight

Think of your intention with love now. You don't need to create it over and over again, as it is the letting go stage of the process. From here on, when you bring your intention into focus allow it to light up and fly away.

Having true compassion and empathy for others is different than feeling pity for them and their circumstances. We are on the journey of self-actualisation and this means that we can't honestly take someone else's power away and still maintain our own sense of personal responsibility.

When we look at someone else's struggle it is easy to say, 'poor you' and judge them as a victim, but this isn't going to work for you anymore—not if you really want to claim your deliberate creation powers.

From now on, you need to see everyone as a powerful mover and shaker. Yes, some may be more lost or be experiencing more hardship—but the closer you focus on the hardship and the struggle the more you grow that within yourself and encourage the continuation of it in the world as a whole.

If this means you need to turn off the news for a while and spend time creating your own reality instead of believing in the one you are seeing, then do it. When you have established the energy of strength and integrity and mastery in your own mind, you will be able to look upon others' experiences and see that they have strength and power too. It is also good to remember that your perception of someone else's reality is far different from their perception of it.

Your perception of reality—in a deep, psychological sense—may only be a figment of your imagination. This is a far-out philosophy, but it deserves consideration. Especially when the world as you see it so clearly transforms as you transform your thinking.

Upon shifting your focus from fear to love, you will notice the external struggles disperse, the pain lessens, the experiences, and the people around us can begin to change dramatically.

As you transform yourself and give in to the beauty of who you are, you will allow yourself to have the peace and the enlightenment you desire.

A Prosperous Flow of Inspired Ideas

How many ideas do we have in a day?

An abundance of intelligence flows through us and onto the page, into the world.

Our imagination lights up in an explosive firework display of weird ideas, new ideas, old ideas, colourful ideas, successful ideas, and the seeds of ideas.

A rich array of ideas are ours for the plucking, flowing through the ether, finding their way into over seven billion minds around the world and that's just the ideas we are aware of.

We are swimming in an ocean of ideas!

We are wealthy with ideas, rich with ideas, we are abundant with ideas!

HEY here comes one now!

Journal Your Thoughts

Q. What does compassion feel like to you?

"Paying attention at every moment, forms a new relationship to time. In some magical way, by slowing down, you become more efficient, productive, and energetic, focusing without distraction directly on the task in front of you. Not only do you become immersed in the moment, you become that moment."

Michael Ray

Day Twenty-nine

Think of your intention with love now. You don't need to create it over and over again, as it is the letting go stage of the process. From here on, when you bring your intention into focus allow it to light up and fly away.

Forgiveness is an interesting word and one of the keys to manifesting a life you really wish to live.

Lack of the forgiveness is a particular energy; it feels like resentment, burning, hardness, anger and so on. These feelings cause confusion in the body and are begging to be processed.

Intense emotions are a way for the body/spirit to call attention to our vibrational set point on certain issues and if we can take the small amount of time as they surface, to sit with them and allow them to have their say without becoming distracted by the story, we will be able to process them.

This is how true forgiveness is born.

Saying the words, 'I AM Willing to forgive and be free,' is a powerful intention. Even if you need to go slowly to process the emotion of all your old hurts and set a new vantage point for deliberate creation, you are still well along the way.

As the pains surface, and you feel like lashing out in blame at the person or experience, do your best to let yourself focus on the physicality of the feeling rather than to rehash the story.

Repeat to yourself, 'even though I feel angry and hurt, I AM willing to forgive and be free.' Use your own words—ones that feel right for you. Being free is your main goal—it needs to take precedence over making someone else pay even when you know they deserve it. If it doesn't, look closely at why you might prefer to live in the pain and discomfort of anger rather than pursue you natural right to live in peace and harmony.

Feel The Flow

Abundance is like sunshine.
Abundance is moonlight.
Abundance is life!

I AM ABUNDANCE!
I cannot separate from the prosperity I AM.

I am here to experience—and if it is gold I want to experience,
then that is what I will experience.

As I soften and take the resistance and fear out of my financial thoughts,
I see immediate improvement.

I clearly hold more gold,
the coins tinkle in my pocket,
people gift me when I least expect it.

I am shown opportunity after opportunity to experience a sense of abundance.
As I let go, more and more it turns magically into dollars and cents.

I embrace the abundance of sunshine.

I allow the broader seeing version of myself to take the reins and show me abundance in
ways I never would have expected to the highest good of all!

Journal Your Thoughts

Q. In order of significance, list 6 things that stand between you and the abundance you wish to experience.

"Silence is not an absence but a presence."

Anne D. LeClaire

Day Thirty

Think of your intention with love now. You don't need to create it over and over again, as it is the letting go stage of the process. From here on, when you bring your intention into focus allow it to light up and fly away.

The vibrational core of you is what interests you now—not the stories, not the past, and not the future.

Now that you know the future is taken care of by the most aware part of yourself, your only job is to focus in on your emotions—feeling around and adjusting the emotional dial to the channel that feels sweetest.

You are sending signals to your perfect knowing universe and this universal aspect of yourself is arranging your life according to that vibrational tone.

Every step along your way is perfectly aligned with the energy you transmit and holds gifts beyond measure.

The feelings of calm, joy, excitement, love, warmth, connection, etc. are the ones you are looking for. Imagine yourself living/looking/being exactly as you wish to be.

Remember that the knowing aspect of our-self has a much broader vision than we do with our little brains and human style limitations—but we can hand it over and repeat our affirmations of self-love and willingness.

We can come back to the now a thousand times a day and have faith that it is well taken care of. We can do our bit by concentrating on feeling our feelings and living our dreams.

Throughout your day, look at your options and pick the one that you most want to do and then inject as much presence and conscious appreciation into it as you can.

I promise before long your life will take on miraculous proportions and you will be one of the 'lucky' ones. Because by now you know that you already are!

A Wealth of Triumphant Thoughts

Thoughts are so abundant we can hardly control them.

We learn to stem the current of thoughts that flow through us and around us and inside us.

Thoughts are wonderful templates of new experiences.
Beautiful, engaging, poetry of thought, tributaries of thought leading in new directions.

Baskets of thoughts, thoughts growing like flowers, blossoming all around us.

A powerful mind, sifting through an abundance of thought, festivals of people having
thoughts, everywhere we go thoughts transforming into things!

Yes, this life is wealthy with thought-forms, miraculous and sparkling,
a never-ending supply of fantastic thoughtfulness!

Journal Your Thoughts

Q. Are you willing to continue to change your mindset? Can you feel the difference of emotion in your body now at the end of the thirty days?

"What the mind can conceive, it can achieve."

Napoleon Hill

Prosperity Consciousness 101
a few key points

Appreciation

When we are little, we are taught to say please and thank you—even when we don't feel grateful. Then as we grow, we are told that appreciation is key to attracting or creating more of what we want in life. But we have been trained to associate the specific words of appreciation with a deadened kind of rote response. Even the word 'grateful' has a twinge of admonishment about it—'Be grateful for what you have!'

Yet appreciation is love in action, a natural response; it is seen in a smile and felt in the body. The more we let ourselves off the hook for not finding the 'right' words—and go back, like a small child, to noticing our body response—the quicker we will return to true appreciation.

Now or Never

I will do it when... I'll feel better later... when my ship comes in... only an hour till I finish work...

What if time doesn't pass?

I worked out that, to a large extent, I was living for the future—waiting, wanting, wishing, and hoping. But once I tuned in to this—ooooohhhh!—it was a terrible feeling.

Then I began whispering to myself, 'this is it, this is it'—and it brought relief.

I'm sure now it's the Zen way—not only committing to this present moment, now—but feeling the sensations in the body and all around us. Without taking stock of our lives in this moment, I think we keep our future manifestations out of reach.

But by being present and saying 'I created this' 'this is it' and 'this is how it feels' we acknowledge and process our lives in present time, clearing the mind and opening doors for different choices making for a different potentially much more satisfying manifestation of the future.

Doing it easy!

When things feel hard, it IS hard!

Life IS Hard when you feel hard/stressed/tight/resistant because you are LIFE. You are feeling your life as you have created it thus far.

Resistance equals sadness and fear, and these qualities make it difficult to appreciate anything.

Here is where 'money doesn't make you happy' comes in.

When you learn to soften to life circumstances, then little things are highlighted and you can again appreciate what you have. You will find that money—like sunshine, smiles, and the stars—can and will make you happy.

Because now life is softer, you are soft, and you are life.

"Listen to the compass of your heart. All you need lies within you."

Mary Anne Radmacher

Thank you so much for taking this journey with me!

If you enjoyed the experience, please consider writing a brief review
on Amazon and/or Goodreads!

We have a lot of cool things in the works, so be sure to follow @arnabaartzartist and
@girlgodbooks on social media – and sign up for our newsletter at
www.thegirlgod.com.

What's Next?

The Seven Goddesses I AM – Arna Baartz

The Crone Initiation and Invitation: Women Speak on the Menopause Journey – Edited by Kay Louise Aldred, Trista Hendren, and Pat Daly

Rainbow Goddess – Celebrating Neurodiversity – Edited by Kay Louise Aldred, Tamara Albanna, Trista Hendren, and Pat Daly

Women's Sovereignty and Body Autonomy Beyond Roe v. Wade – Edited by Arlene Bailey, Pat Daly, Sharon Smith, and Trista Hendren

Kali Rising: Sacred Rage – Edited by C. Ara Campbell, Jaclyn Cherie, Pat Daly, and Trista Hendren

Pain Perspectives: Finding Meaning in the Fire – Edited by Kay Louise Aldred, Trista Hendren, and Pat Daly

Making Love with the Divine: Sacred, Ecstatic, Erotic Experiences – Kay Louise Aldred

Embodied Education – Kay Louise Aldred and Dan Aldred

Songs of Solstice: Goddess Carols – Edited by Trista Hendren, Sharon Smith, and Pat Daly

Goddess Chants and Songs Book – Edited by Trista Hendren, Anique Radiant Heart, and Pat Daly

Lotus Heart: The Compassion of Kuan Yin – Edited by Trista Hendren, Herng Yu Tzong, and Yeshe Matthews

And Still, I Rise – Kat Shaw

Other: Anthologies and children's books on the Black Madonna, Mary Magdalene, Mother Mary, Aradia, Kali, Brigid, Sophia, Spider Woman, Persephone and Hecate are also in the works.

http://thegirlgod.com/publishing.php